IN ORDER TO KNOW GOD

A 40-day Devotional for Queer Christians to Help Build a Closer Relationship with God

YEAMAH LOGAN

Copyright © 2023 Yeamah Logan

All rights reserved. This book or any portion thereof may not be reproduced or used in any many whatsoever without the express written permission of the publisher except for the use of brief quotations in a book review.

Printed in the United States of America

First Printing, 2017

ISBN Print: 978-0-9993642-2-2

ISBN Kindle: 978-0-9993642-3-9

Naked Diamond LLC Publishing
2295 New Center Point #1067
Colorado Springs, CO 80922

www.yeamah.com

Information on special discounts for bulk purchases, sales, promotions, fundraising, and educational needs contact hello@yeamah.com

All scriptures are NIV unless otherwise referenced.
Copyright 2023 Naked Diamond LLC Publishing
Published June 2023

Table of Contents

Introduction v

The Feelings of God

Day 1	The Dance of Love 1
Day 2	The Power of Love 3
Day 3	The Goodness of Love 5
Day 4	Love's Acceptance & Celebration 7
Day 5	God is Love 9
Day 6	God is Kind 11
Day 7	God is Gentle 13
Day 8	God is Passionate 15
Day 9	The Passion of Christ 17
Day 10	God is Compassionate 19

The Ways of God

Day 11	God Never Leaves You 21
Day 12	God Guides Your Path 23
Day 13	God Holds Your Future 25
Day 14	God Values You as Precious 27
Day 15	God Gives Only Good Gifts 29
Day 16	God Provides for You 31
Day 17	God's Love is Unconditional 33
Day 18	God Perfects Your Life 35

Day 19	God Sees You as Righteous	37
Day 20	God Deems You Worthy	39

The Actions of God

Day 21	God as Protector	41
Day 22	God as Provider	43
Day 23	God as Healer	45
Day 24	God is a Mental Health Healer	47
Day 25	God Comforts Us	49
Day 26	God a Servant	51
Day 27	God as Teacher	53
Day 28	God as Celebrator	55
Day 29	God as Deliverer	57
Day 30	Jesus is the Word of God.	59

The Words of God

Day 31	Words of Love	61
Day 32	Words of Inclusion	63
Day 33	Words of Forgiveness	65
Day 34	Words of Encouragement	67
Day 35	Words of Humility	69
Day 36	Words of Faith	71
Day 37	Words of Peace	73
Day 38	Words of Wholeness	75
Day 39	Words of Freedom	77
Day 40	Words of Oneness	79
About the Author		81

Introduction

The purpose of this devotional is to provide guidance and support for LGBTQ+ Christians to develop a deep connection with God. These pages are written to draw you closer to God and build a stronger relationship. While it is recommended that you read each daily meditation and practice in the morning, it is not required.

Knowing the character and nature of God is crucial to living out your faith as an LGBTQ+ Christian. Without this knowledge, it can be difficult to discern the voice of God from the voice of non-affirming sources. Therefore, it is essential to learn the voice of God.

Upon completing this devotional, don't hesitate to start over from day one with a renewed mind and a fresh perspective. God is always ready to take you higher and deeper in the knowledge of Himself.

Note that in this devotional, God will be referred to as God and not as Goddess, Source, Consciousness, or Infinite Intelligence. However, if these terms resonate with you, feel free to cross out the term God and replace it with your preferred name for God. The pronouns used for God will alternate between He/Her/They/Them.

This book is written in a Christian framework to be read alongside the Bible, so the pronoun He will be used. Nevertheless, feel free to substitute this pronoun with one that resonates more with you. God is not offended, and neither am I.

Some days, we will meditate on a particular scripture, while other days, we will discuss an aspect of God in general.

Let's begin!

DAY 1

The Dance of Love

Place me like a seal over your heart, like a seal on your arm; for love is as strong as death, its jealousy unyielding as the grave. It burns like blazing fire, like a mighty flame. Many waters cannot quench love; rivers cannot sweep it away. If one were to give all the wealth of one's house for love, it would be utterly scorned.
Song of Solomon 8:6-7

Love is certain in life as death, and even stronger because it exists beyond death. This scripture comes in the middle of a discourse between two lovers, with this verse being the feminine's directive to her masculine counterpart. These two energies are in constant lovers' dance within ourselves and in the world at large.

We are always engaged in the dance of love with the feminine and masculine aspects of ourselves. The love between these two energies is passionate and intense, not always calm, although it has its moments. The feminine and masculine are always yearning to become one, to achieve wholeness with each other.

This is true for everyone, regardless of gender expression or sexual orientation.
Love is the force that calls to you today and every day. It never diminishes, regardless of your behavior, attitudes, or thoughts. All it requires is for you to place it as a seal over your heart, to receive it.

Practice:

Take a moment to read the above scripture. Choose an image online that represents a part of the verse that stood out to you today. Use that image as your phone screensaver for the rest of the week to remind you of the passionate and jealous presence of love that calls to you in every moment of every day.

DAY 2

The Power of Love

And so, we know and rely on the love God has for us. God is love. Whoever lives in love lives in God, and God in them. This is how love is made complete among us so that we will have confidence on the day of judgment: In this world we are like Jesus. There is no fear in love. But perfect love drives out fear because fear has to do with punishment. The one who fears is not made perfect in love.
1 John 4:16-18

Love and fear cannot coexist in the same space. Love is greater than fear, and wherever love is, fear is repelled. Conversely, where there is fear, there is no love.

As a queer believer, you may have grown accustomed to fear being a normal part of your relationship with God. However, according to the scripture above, fear is evidence that we are not in a true relationship with God.

The Power of Love

The perfect love of God drives out fear. The scripture says that if we have fear, we have not been made perfect in love. How do we become perfect in love? By receiving God's love in our hearts and minds and having faith that God loves us unconditionally.

This process must be done by faith, as our brains and society constantly give us reasons not to believe that God loves us unconditionally. We must actively receive God's love, not just understand it, in order to become perfect in love. After receiving it, the understanding will come. That's the formula.

Psalm 34:4 says, "I sought the Lord, and he answered me; he delivered me from all my fears."

Practice:

Write in your journal 30 times, "I receive God's love for me." Say it to yourself throughout the day, whenever you pick up your phone to scroll on social media or check emails. Let this practice help you overcome fear and embrace the power of God's unconditional love.

DAY 3

The Goodness of Love

> *Taste and see that the LORD is good;*
> *blessed is the one who takes refuge in*
> *him. Fear the LORD, you his holy people,*
> *for those who fear him lack nothing.*
> *Psalm 34:8-9*

God's love is not a fake religious cover-up for punishment and pain. It is good, according to the dictionary's definition of good, not the church's definition.

Good (n): Benefit or advantage to someone or something.

God's love is beneficial and advantageous to you today, like the kind of good a child can recognize. It is the kind of good that remains good even after scrutiny and analysis. This type of goodness translates across all cultures and timelines. The point is clear: God's love is genuinely good.

Therefore, today's meditation and encouragement is to acknowledge that God's goodness has been complicated and twisted into a religious construct that even God cannot recognize. God's goodness is something that can be recognized by our five senses - something we can taste and see - meaning it's tangible. And it is tangible today!

Practice:

Take a moment to meditate on the tangible goodness of God's love. Acknowledge and appreciate its benefits and advantages in your life. Allow this realization to bring you peace and joy.

DAY 4

Love's Acceptance & Celebration

> *The LORD your God is with you, the Mighty Warrior who saves. He will take great delight in you; in his love he will no longer rebuke you but will rejoice over you with singing.*
> *Zephaniah 3:17*

The phrase "rejoice over you" literally means "dance, skip, leap, and spin around in joy." Just picture God dancing, skipping, leaping, and spinning around in joy because of how God loves you. Take a moment and pause to catch that image, regardless of the image of God that you have in your mind, even if it's still the old white guy with a long beard.

If you really take the time to do that, you're experiencing a small portion of how God feels about you. It's quite overwhelming, isn't it?

As a queer believer, you must understand that God is not in the business of rebuking you. Even Jesus said in John 3:17 that He did not come to condemn you or me, but to save us. That word "save" is sozo, and if you've been in the church for a while, you know that word means to make you whole, to make sure there's nothing missing or lacking in your life, and to make you complete.

The idea of needing to earn God's acceptance or prove your worth to God can be swallowed up by this scripture. Your job in this relationship with God is to RECEIVE and ENJOY this love. Your job is to join in the celebration of who you are. God is no longer having a conversation with you about acceptance. You are already accepted, and it's time to celebrate!

Practice:

Spend some time frolicking wherever you feel comfortable and picture God there doing it with you. Or do something to celebrate yourself, like having a mini birthday party with just you and God. Order ice cream or go to the store and buy yourself a birthday cake. Join God in the celebration of you!

DAY 5

God is Love

> *Love is patient, love is kind. It does not envy, it does not boast, it is not proud. It does not dishonour others, it is not self-seeking, it is not easily angered, it keeps no record of wrongs. Love does not delight in evil but rejoices with the truth. It always protects, always trusts, always hopes, always perseveres. Love never fails. But where there are prophecies, they will cease; where there are tongues, they will be stilled; where there is knowledge, it will pass away.*
> *1 Corinthians 13:4-8*

Beloved, have you ever felt burdened by the pressure to perform well as a Christian? Maybe you've heard the phrase "how is your love walk?" and felt overwhelmed by the idea of having to love perfectly. But here's the truth: 1 Corinthians 13:4-8 isn't a checklist or to-do list for you to follow. Rather, it's a description of who God is.

According to 1 John 4:16, God is love. So when you read those verses, you can replace the word "love" with "God" and see a beautiful portrait of the nature and character of God. This means that God is patient and kind, not envious or boastful, not arrogant or rude. God does not insist on having His own way and is not irritable or resentful. God rejoices in truth, bears all things, believes all things, hopes all things, and endures all things.

So when you face challenges and difficulties in your day, remember that God is not punishing you or keeping a record of your wrongs. Rather, God is always thinking the best about you and has plans to prosper you. You can be certain that you and God are on very good terms.

Practice:

Take some time today to rewrite 1 Corinthians 13:4-8 in your journal, replacing "love" with "God." Then, read it out loud three times throughout the day, in the morning, afternoon, and evening. Let the truth of who God is sink deeply into your heart and mind, and let it bring you peace and comfort.

DAY 6

God is Kind

Love is patient, love is kind.
1 Corinthian 13:4

I remember the first day I realized that God was kind to me. It took me an entire week to calm down from that high. And that's why we are giving this its own day. The kindness of God is often overlooked for greater and deeper spiritual truths, but this is one of the most revolutionary aspects of God in our current society.

Kindness is in short supply. We are not kind to ourselves, our families, coworkers, partners, and even sometimes our dogs. We do random acts of kindness because we don't understand that kindness is an attitude and a way of looking at the world.

The beautiful thing about kindness is that it has no expectations of the recipient. The kindest thing we can do is to speak well of something or someone, and that includes ourselves. The reason this was so revolutionary for me was because God's kindness gave me permission to be kinder to myself. To cut myself some slack and release the impossible standards I set for myself.

God is Kind

God's kindness is described in the Bible as "hesed," which means loving-kindness. In Psalm 36:7-9, the psalmist speaks of God's "abundance of loving-kindness." When we experience God's kindness, we are experiencing an overflow of his love.

Is your inner voice kind to you?

Practice:

Be intentional today and pay attention to how many unkind things you say to yourself, even if you're joking. And then at the end of the day, decide if you would like to change that if necessary. Then write 30 kind things about yourself. Remember that God's kindness extends to you, and you are worthy of being kind to yourself as well.

DAY 7

God is Gentle

He tends his flock like a shepherd:
He gathers the lambs in his arms and
carries them close to his heart; he
gently leads those that have young.
Isaiah 40:11

God's parenting style is often described as gentle, like that of a loving mother or father with their child. It's the kind of parenting that doesn't involve yelling or shaming, but rather correction that reminds you of your identity and separates it from your actions. Even when Scripture speaks of God chastising those He loves, it's not a wicked punishment, but rather a loving correction.

The goodness of God is what brings us to repentance, and it's the kindness and miracles that Jesus performed that caused people to turn towards Him. So, rest assured that God is not out to get you. Whenever you approach God, you will always be met with open arms and compassionate listening.

God is Gentle

Practice:

Take a moment to visualize yourself walking up to God and seeing Him stoop down to your level, looking you in the eye as you share your plans for the day. If you're doing this exercise at the end of the day, reflect on how your day went and share it with God.

DAY 8

God is Passionate

> *Do you think the Scriptures have no meaning? They say that God is passionate that the spirit he has placed within us should be faithful to him.*
> *James 4:5 NLT*

God is so passionate about you that James says God lusts after you. James 4:5 KJV.

Passion is felt and experienced as an almost uncontrollable desire, which in the church has been synonymous with lust. And has been used to describe what LGB people are guilty of. We've been accused of having uncontrollable desire and out of control passions, but here in James it says God does also.

It says God lusts after us, that God is so passionate about us it feels almost uncontrollable.

Therefore, passion is Godly.

Your passion for your partner or your crush is not evidence of the devil or anything evil on the inside of you. It is only evidence that you indeed are made in the image of God.

It's important also to note, passion is an **almost** uncontrollable desire. Not an actual uncontrollable desire. Passion becomes poison when we do not exercise self-control, which leads to things that harm other people and ourselves.

So if you've felt passion for a person of the same gender it is not wrong or sinful. It is normal to feel passionate about people who are important to you and who you love. That passion can be controlled and expressed in healthy ways that are good for you and the other person equally.

Practice:

Write down 10 synonyms of the word passion and see in what other areas of your life you've experienced passion and expressed it in a healthy way.

DAY 9

The Passion of Christ

For God so loved the world that
he gave his one and only Son, that
whoever believes in him shall not
perish but have eternal life.
John 3:16

God's passion is often taught through the suffering and sacrifice of Christ. It's no wonder there's a movie called the Passion of Christ that shows us the depth of His love. However, we can get so fixated on the crucifixion that we forget it was for the joy set before Him that Jesus endured the cross. (Hebrews 12:2) The true passion wasn't the cross, but rather the resurrection and His desire for a relationship with you.

Jesus didn't just come to die so that we could wallow in self-pity and feel bad about ourselves. On the contrary, He died so that we could see how much we are worth, not how worthless. The cross was meant to remove every limiting belief that we have about God or ourselves that stands in the way of a relationship with Him.

The cross was a way of silencing our perfectionism and reminding us that we cannot earn our salvation. Jesus says, "Please just accept my love and come closer. I want to know you." (John 17:3) The cross was a powerful mirror that reflects not our sins, but our immeasurable worth in God's eyes.

Practice:

Remember that Jesus got off the cross so that you could too. Today, imagine yourself in Christ walking away from the cross and ascending with Him. (Colossians 3:1)

DAY 10

God is Compassionate

> *For we do not have a high priest who is unable to empathize with our weaknesses, but we have one who has been tempted in every way, just as we are—yet he did not sin. Let us then approach God's throne of grace with confidence, so that we may receive mercy and find grace to help us in our time of need.*
> *Hebrews 4:15-16*

God not only sympathizes with everything you go through, but because of Jesus, God also empathizes with you. There's nothing you're experiencing right now that God doesn't understand - the ins and outs, the emotions, the intrusive thoughts, the merry-go-round thoughts, all of it.

God's compassion towards you should give you the confidence to come to Him whenever and however you want. You can be sure that God is never judging you because He understands the roots of all your pain and hurt, and He's always ready to heal you. (Psalm 34:18)

God is Compassionate

Whenever you need help, God's compassion is there, ready for you to draw from. It's a well that never runs dry. God's compassion can never be exhausted or emptied, and you have an entire lifetime, maybe even two, to spend the compassion God has set aside for you.

The most beautiful part is that God actually wants you to draw on His compassion. He wants you to come and receive His mercy and grace. You don't even have to convince God that you're worthy of it - He just says, "Come, I got it in abundance until infinity, how much do you need today?"

Practice:

Google the Niagara Falls and find a video of the water flowing. Then, assign God's compassion to that water and picture yourself in the midst of the falls, receiving all of God's compassion whenever you're ready or needing it. It will never run dry.

DAY 11

God Never Leaves You

> *The LORD himself goes before you
> and will be with you; he will never
> leave you nor forsake you. Do not
> be afraid; do be not discouraged.*
> *Deuteronomy 3:18*

The thought of leaving you has never crossed the mind of God. It has never occurred to God to desert you and leave you to figure out life on your own. God is intimately aware and invested in who you are, what you do, and the people you are in a relationship with, including romantic relationships.

You are not an afterthought. While God promises to never leave you, the greater statement is that God will always be present. You will always be on God's mind. Even when circumstances arise that tempt you to believe God has somehow turned His back on you, Scripture confirms many times that it will never happen.

You can rest assured.

The cliche that the Teacher is silent during the test as a way to explain why we may not be able to hear the voice of God through trying times is not in alignment with the character of God. In fact, Scripture says He is an ever-present help in times of trouble and is close to the brokenhearted.

There's no test, and the Teacher lives within you, and He can never think about leaving or forsaking you. God's thoughts are firmly rested on you today, beloved. Can you sense it?

Practice:

Throughout your day today, however you picture the person of Jesus, I want you to picture Jesus always with you. For example, picture Jesus in the passenger seat, or across the dining table, or next to you in your cubicle or office, or waiting outside the bathroom door for you. See Jesus with you always today. Psalm 139:17-18.

DAY 12

God Guides Your Path

> *But as it is written, Eye hath not seen, nor ear heard, neither have entered into the heart of man, the things which God hath prepared for them that love him.*
> *1 Corinthians 2:9*

A plan that you will enjoy and easily find if you follow your heart. Isn't that awesome? God built in you the blueprint of those plans. And made your desires in such a way that they align with the plan. He didn't want you searching outside of yourself for that plan, so He put it in your desires.

You have a built-in blueprint for your life, designed by God just for you. You may be thinking, "Well, so far this blueprint sucks!" And you are probably right. Here's why:

Our society does a really great job teaching us how not to trust ourselves and our desires. They teach us not to follow our hearts because our hearts are desperately wicked. But what they have missed is that God has placed our blueprint in our hearts. We were created to follow our heart into the perfect plan for our lives, designed by God Himself.

So, life may suck right now, but it can begin to get better today simply by aligning your thoughts with the thoughts of God for you. Scripture says, "For who knows a person's thoughts except their own spirit within them? In the same way, no one knows the thoughts of God except the Spirit of God" (1 Corinthians 2:11, NIV). That means you have the mind of Christ, and you can discern His will for your life.

Practice:

Set your timer for 10 minutes. Get your journal and begin to write all of the desires of your heart, WITHOUT judgment! It doesn't matter what that desire is; pour everything you can think of and sense onto the paper or papers. When you're complete, read it out loud to God and write down anything you hear or sense in your heart from God.

Then I want you to put this phrase before all of the desires you wrote down and read it out loud. "[Your name], I God want you to [insert desire]."

DAY 13

God Holds Your Future

*For I know the thoughts that I
think toward you, saith the LORD,
thoughts of peace, and not of evil,
to give you an expected end.
Jeremiah 29:11 KJV*

This includes eternity. God's plan for you does not include hell. I think we can end the day right there, right? But let's get really clear on this.

God's thoughts about you are not focused on eternal punishment; it's not even focused on present-day punishment. God's thoughts of you are filled with things that will prosper you, situations that will bless you, and be good to you. And God is not hiding those thoughts from you.

Moreover, it is not a surprise. It is an expected end. You are expected, by God, to spend eternity in a relationship with Him. So, if you've ever worried whether you'll reach the end of your life and be surprised where you end up, this scripture tells you it is not possible.

God's thoughts about your future, dearly beloved, do not include hell.

Practice:

Write that statement in your journal as many times as you can in 3 minutes and put your name in it.

"God's plan for me, [insert name], does not include hell." (John 3:16-17, Jeremiah 29:11)"

DAY 14

God Values You as Precious

> *Indeed, the very hairs of your head are*
> *all numbered. Don't be afraid; you are*
> *worth more than many sparrows.*
> *Matthew 6:26*

God sees your value. God thinks of you as valuable and worthy. You do not lose value in the eyes or mind of God, ever.

Your value is intrinsic. It is not based on your actions. You do not become less valuable because you behave unlovingly. You are still valuable. Remember what the scripture says: "But God demonstrates his own love for us in this: While we were still sinners, Christ died for us." (Romans 5:8) It wasn't after we got it together and then God saw our value. No, it was while we were behaving less than the image of God that God showed up.

Your value is intrinsic. Yes, I am repeating myself. This truth is worth repeating a thousand times over. The absence of this truth is what makes you think God isn't answering your prayer because you "messed up" or because you have a crush on that person or are in a relationship with a person of the same gender.

28 God Values You as Precious

As a person who has intrinsic value, your prayers are always worth it to God. God always wants to listen to you because your thoughts are valuable to God. Your feelings are valuable to God. Your plans are valuable to God. Everything about you is precious and dear to God.

Practice:

Think of the thing you value the most. Feel in your heart how intensely you value that thing or person. Now, see God feeling and viewing you in the same way. Remind yourself throughout the day, "My value is intrinsic."

DAY 15

God Gives Only Good Gifts

> *Praise be to the God and Father*
> *of our Lord Jesus Christ, who has*
> *blessed us in the heavenly realms with*
> *every spiritual blessing in Christ.*
> *Ephesians 1:3*

God's first thoughts about you every day are how to bless you. It is not to punish you or afflict you with sickness. Such notions are not only weird but also unscriptural. As we read in Genesis, God's first words to mankind were words of blessing. This suggests that God's heart is full of blessings, and He constantly thinks of ways to bless us.

It would benefit you to fill your heart with thoughts of God's blessings. Remember that when you speak, whether to yourself or others, you should speak blessings over yourself, just like God does.

Practice:

Get some sticky notes and write blessings on them, then put them on your bathroom mirror or somewhere private where you can see them every day.

Bible verse reference: "The Lord bless you and keep you; the Lord make his face shine on you and be gracious to you; the Lord turn his face toward you and give you peace" (Numbers 6:24-26, NIV)."

DAY 16

God Provides for You

> *And God is able to bless you*
> *abundantly, so that in all things at all*
> *times, having all that you need, you*
> *will abound in every good work.*
> *2 Corinthians 9:8*

Prosperity means to flourish financially. Money can be a sensitive topic, especially in relation to church and tithing. We may feel obligated to give and believe that feeling guilty when we don't give is the Holy Spirit convicting us. We are often told that if giving to the church does not hurt us, it means we did not give enough to activate God's generosity and prosperity. However, this message is not reflective of the pattern seen in Scripture or God's thoughts toward us.

The pattern in Scripture is that God gives first. God is generous first. God prospers first. And then, only then, out of our abundance are we able to give cheerfully, as Paul states is the will of God. God fills us to overflow and desires us to give from that overflow.

Prospering financially is not a taboo subject to God. In fact, God wants us to prosper financially so that we can be a blessing to others. How else can we be a blessing if we are not blessed or prospered by God? It's impossible. While we can be generous with our time and prayers, the world also needs their physical needs met. God knows this, and asks us not to worry about them, not because we don't need them, but because He has already made up His mind to meet them. It's not a prayer point if it's something that is automatically ours.

Practice:

If any of the above triggers feelings of lack or anger, take the time to be curious about those emotions. Take out your journal and draw two columns. On the right side, label it "What I Believe About God and Money," and on the left side, "What God Says About Money." List your beliefs and throughout the day, be open to answers or responses from God in conversations, TV shows, work tasks, or quiet moments.

DAY 17

God's Love is Unconditional

> *To me this is like the days of Noah*
> *when I swore that the waters of Noah*
> *would never again cover the earth.*
> *So now I have sworn not to be angry*
> *with you, never to rebuke you again.*
> Isaiah 54:9

Have you ever thought, "I hope God's not mad at me?" Have you ever received a pang of guilt or fear because you felt God must be angry or disappointed in you? Well, the Scripture says that is impossible. God has never and will never be angry with you, on this side of the Cross.

Those feelings are actually from the enemy. However, you interpret evil in the world, as the wrong beliefs you were taught in church, or an actual entity whose sole purpose is to make us suffer – guilt, shame, and condemnation come from it. It does not come from God.

God is never angry with you, beloved. God loves you sincerely and is always kind towards you. God is always merciful and compassionate. Here's why? God knows you better than you know yourself. God remembers your past better than you do. God knows why you behave the way you do. God was there when you first believed a lie about yourself, that you were not worthy or deserving. God knows the root of your misstep or "mistake" and wants to heal you and call you into the fullness of who you are.

The anger of God is not what heals or brings to repentance. As a matter of fact, Scripture says it is the goodness of God that brings us to repentance (Romans 2:4). Meaning it is God's goodness, not anger, that helps us change our minds about who we are so we can align our actions with the highest versions of ourselves.

Practice:

Set your timer for 5 minutes. Sit with your eyes closed and picture God however you see God in your imagination. Now see God with an enormous smile on God's face. Sit there and feel what it's like to have God smile over you and with you. Take that image throughout your day today. Whenever you have a free moment, see God smiling.

DAY 18

God Perfects Your Life

*The Lord will perfect that which concerns
me; Your mercy and loving-kindness,
O Lord, endure forever—forsake not
the works of Your own hands.*
Psalm 138:8 AMPC

All the things in your life that you think are too trivial for God to be concerned about are actually on His mind. And not just on His mind, but actively being perfected and made complete by Him. Does that sound too good to be true?

It's not.

As you look back through your life, you can see how supernatural and miraculous things have happened for you in both the most intimate and public areas of your life.

The concerns you have about how people are going to treat you as an LGBTQIA+ person, the worries you have about your family beliefs and the church--God is in it with you. It is on God's mind. Your coming out plan, if you haven't already, is on the mind of God. Your fears are on His mind.

God shares your concerns, but more than that, He wants you to give those concerns to Him (1 Peter 5:7). God's way of perfecting that which concerns you is to eliminate those concerns by giving them up to Him.

God is able to organize those concerns for you and provide a way out or through those concerns.

Practice:

What concerns about your journey have you been holding onto, thinking they were not important to God? Make a list of those and on top of that list, write "NOT MY CONCERN". Then, release the responsibility to God. Do this as many times as you need to.

DAY 19

God Sees You as Righteous

> *God made him who had no sin to be*
> *sin for us, so that in him we might*
> *become the righteousness of God.*
> *2 Corinthians 5:21*

Did you know that in God's eyes, you are as sinless as Jesus is? It may sound too good to be true, but the Bible supports this truth. Here are a few verses to back it up: Romans 3:22, 2 Corinthians 5:21, and 1 Peter 2:24. Take some time to read and reflect on these verses.

You are not a sinner, but rather you are righteous and spotless in God's sight, no matter your sexual orientation, gender identity, or relationship status. Hebrews 10:14 confirms this: "For by one sacrifice he has made perfect forever those who are being made holy."

You are perfect. You are holy. You are righteous.

Living in this truth can be transformative. Imagine the freedom and joy you could experience if you truly believed that you are a righteous and beloved child of God. You are enough and loved just as you are.

Practice:

Write in your journal 33 times, "I am a righteous [insert how you identify] person. I agree with God." Allow this truth to sink in and shape your self-image.

DAY 20

God Deems You Worthy

See, I have engraved you on the palms of
my hands; your walls are ever before me.
Isaiah 49:16

God is always thinking about you–and everyone else. It's a God thing, and we can't wrap our minds around it, but it is true.

You mean so much to God. God cannot value you more than He does at this moment. And in the next moment. And in every moment to come! The full weight of God's value of you is present in all and each of your moments.

There's never a time when God's attention is off of you. As Psalm 139:1-3 says, "O Lord, you have searched me and known me! You know when I sit down and when I rise up; you discern my thoughts from afar. You search out my path and my lying down and are acquainted with all my ways."

You are important and worthy of God's attention and thoughts, not because He needs to pay attention to you because you're messing up, but because you are a part of God's expression in the world.

God can never hate Godself, and because you are a part of God, God can never hate you or see you less valuable than Himself. You are as worthy to God as God is to Herself.

Practice:

Read Psalm 139 and insert your name into the verses.

DAY 21

God as Protector

> *The LORD is my shepherd, I lack nothing. He makes me lie down in green pastures, he leads me beside quiet waters, he refreshes my soul. He guides me along the right paths for his name's sake. Even though I walk through the darkest valley, I will fear no evil, for you are with me; your rod and your staff, they comfort me.*
> *Psalm 23:1-4*

God protects us not by intervening uninvited in our lives, but by guiding us through an intimate relationship with Him. We often struggle to understand God's protection, especially when we see so much pain and trauma in the world. It's natural to question where God is when we experience childhood trauma or face hate and discrimination as LGBTQ+ people. But God welcomes and encourages these questions (Isaiah 30:21).

The truth is, God is a Protector, but His protection doesn't always look like we expect. He doesn't always intervene or stop bad things from happening. However, God protects us through our relationship with Him and with each other. We have all experienced a nudge to reach out to a friend or ignore a feeling that something isn't right. These are ways in which God protects us.

Psalm 23 paints a beautiful picture of God as our Shepherd, leading us and guiding us. God is a leader, not an intervener. His protection comes through relationship and guidance, not by stepping in and stopping bad things from happening.

Practice:

Today's devotion may have brought up difficult memories or emotions. Take time to journal about these feelings, and use the characteristics of God that you have learned about in the past 20 days to bring your questions and concerns to God. He is loving and kind, and He is waiting to have this conversation with you.

DAY 22

God as Provider

> *And my God will meet all your*
> *needs according to the riches of*
> *his glory in Christ Jesus.*
> *Philippians 4:19*

Today may be another tough day, so buckle up, beloved. Because we are not used to saying out loud that we don't believe God is a Provider, especially if we've struggled in life. Again, where was God?

How does God provide? Through your faith.

God will not suspend natural law and cause money to fall from the sky or magically erect your dream home in your dream location. Unless you have the faith for it, and in that case, all power to your amazing faith, and we welcome all of those miracles!

The truth is, God provides through your faith because everything you would ever need is already available for you in heaven. If you can, imagine a heavenly vault that was created on the day you transitioned to Earth, with everything you would ever need financially. This vault has been available to you from the moment you arrived on Earth.

Or how about considering the story of the Garden of Eden? When were Adam and Eve created? They were created after the Earth was abundant and filled with everything they could possibly need. If God can do it for them, beloved, you are no different. Your life is no less important. You have the same access to abundance as Adam and Eve, King Solomon, and Jesus.

As a matter of fact, Scripture says you are a joint-heir with Christ. (Romans 8:17) Notice, this is nothing you did to earn it. You were born into it. You are an heir by birth and by faith in Jesus Christ. Just like you were born into your beautiful queer identity, you were also born with access to abundance.

Practice:

Find a 10-minute instrumental meditation music on YouTube or another streaming platform. You are going to imagine yourself going into heaven, however you see or imagine heaven. You are going to see yourself going to a large room with endless vaults lined up on both sides. You are going to find yours with your name on a plaque on top of the vault, and I want you with Jesus, however you see Jesus, to open the vault.

DAY 23

God as Healer

> *"He himself bore our sins" in his body on the cross, so that we might die to sins and live for righteousness; "by his wounds you have been healed."*
> *1 Peter 2:24*

Healing can be an uncomfortable topic because we've all had experiences where someone prayed and they weren't healed. You may even have prayed and you weren't healed. This devotional day is not enough space to discuss all of the nuanced ways we can answer those questions, but it is enough space to debunk this idea: God doesn't heal everyone.

It is true, God doesn't heal everyone by intervening into our lives and choosing who to heal and who not to heal. This is because you and I were built to heal. Our bodies were designed to heal themselves. As someone who graduated with a degree in Biology, I can tell you the minute you injure yourself, like cut your finger, your physiology kicks in and begins to heal and close that wound.

The healing is built in.

What about those miracles? What about the people who say they were miraculously healed after prayer? That is true. In circumstances when our bodies' natural defenses are down, our faith in what we are saying will trigger our bodies to restart and begin to heal itself.

Again, the healing is built in.

That Scripture says, "by his wounds, you have been healed" (1 Peter 2:24). It is past tense. Meaning all of the healing you would ever need is already here. It is your faith, your belief, acceptance and surrender to that truth that invites healing into your physical body.

Practice:

In your journal today, write all of your honest thoughts about healing down in a letter to God. Express all of your doubts, fears and maybe even anger as to why there is sickness and disease in the world today. And then take a step back, breathe, and ask God to reveal why the world is in the state of sickness and disease. Take your time and listen. Don't force it.

DAY 24

God is a Mental Health Healer

> *Beloved, I wish above all things*
> *that thou mayest prosper and be in*
> *health, even as thy soul prospereth.*
> *1 John 3:2 KJV*

God has provided not only for the physical healing of our bodies but also for our mental healing and health. There is an unending reservoir of peace available to you today - peace that never ends, that surpasses all understanding, and that never quits. So how do you access it?

The answer is through faith. You are a spiritual being who possesses a mind that controls your body. Your spiritual self is the leader in your life if you allow it to be through faith.

God is not intentionally targeting you or causing fear in your life. He is not letting bad things happen to you so that you experience guilt, shame, or condemnation. The Holy Spirit is not convicting you through pain, shame, guilt, or condemnation.

God wants you to be mentally healthy and whole, and this is evident in Scripture. For instance, 3 John 1:2 says, "Beloved, I pray that in all respects you may prosper and be in good health, just as your soul prospers."

If you can believe that God desires for you to be mentally whole and prospering in your soul, you will experience true peace that surpasses all understanding. Will you believe that today?

Practice:

Answer this question, "Do you believe God desires for you to be mentally whole and prospering in your soul?" Then ask yourself why and keep asking yourself why until you get to the simplest answer. Take that answer with you throughout your day today.

DAY 25

God Comforts Us

Praise be to the God and Father of our Lord Jesus Christ, the Father of compassion and the God of all comfort, who comforts us in all our troubles, so that we can comfort those in any trouble with the comfort we ourselves receive from God.
2 *Corinthians 1:3-4*

Imagine having a really rough day and coming home, crawling up in the comfiest position and having the biggest fluffiest comforter cover you. How would that feel? How would you relax at that moment? How would you let go at that moment?

The comforter has no expectations for you to get over it already, it is not rushing your processes, it's not even telling you to feel the emotions–it's just there. It's present with you. In the moment with you. No expectations and no judgments. That is God as our Comforter.

The Comforter goes further if needed to remind you how beautiful you are, how loved you are, how sacred and holy you are. The Comforter's words are there to ease whatever pain, whatever grief or stress.

This is God. And you have access to this God in every moment of every day. This comforting Presence dwells with you. So beloved, if today you are struggling a little bit to find your good face. If you're struggling to show up for anybody, including yourself, know that God as your Comforter is near. You can rest and lean on God's strength and love today with no agenda.

The Holy Spirit, whom the Father will send in my name, will teach you all things and will remind you of everything I have said to you. Peace I leave with you; my peace I give you. I do not give to you as the world gives. Do not let your hearts be troubled and do not be afraid. - John 14:26-27

Practice:

Find 30 minutes today to lay down. Put some comforting sounds on and just lay down and rest. Even if that time is in your car, recline your seat and lay down. That's it.

DAY 26

God a Servant

> *The greatest among you*
> *will be your servant.*
> *Matthew 23:11*

The greatest leader will always be the greatest servant. Being in service is always done by the greatest person in the room. And in every room, that person is God. As it is written in Mark 10:45, 'For even the Son of Man came not to be served but to serve, and to give his life as a ransom for many.' God is always in active service towards you in the person of the Holy Spirit, Jesus, and Godself.

Think about it this way, the literal meaning of the word ministry is service. Therefore, every day and in every single moment, God is ministering to your needs, desires, and goals. Listening is a ministry. Teaching is ministry. Prophecy is ministry. Giving is ministry. Faith is ministry. You get it. In every way the Spirit of God manifests in us, it is God Himself ministering and serving you.

One of the greatest ways, if not the most powerful ways, of being like God, is to be in service to others around you. But this can only be done when you are clear of the depths of God's service and ministry toward you. We always give out of an overflow of what we've received from God. This means service and ministry are not reserved for the four walls of the church or the soup kitchen. It means service is everywhere you are where there is another human. This human doesn't have to be in need because service is also joining in and sharing the joys of the people around us.

How can you receive the ministry of God today?

Practice:

Read John 13:1-20 and meditate on the lesson Jesus was showing and demonstrating for the disciples. And be intentional today to carry that lesson in your life and choose to be an imitator of God and choose to serve and minister to those around you.

DAY 27

God as Teacher

> *I will instruct you and teach you in the way you should go; I will counsel you with my loving eye on you.*
> *Psalm 32:8*

What a relief it is to know that God is a loving teacher and not a dictator! Contrary to what some may have been taught, God is patient and gentle in His instruction. Unlike a dictator, there is no rush in God's classroom. Each student receives personalized attention and lesson plans tailored to their unique path, style of learning, gifts, and talents.

In God's classroom, there is no competition to be the best learner or score the highest on a morality or spirituality test. Instead, you are being personally guided by your Creator to fulfill your unique design and plan for your life. Your identity, including your queer identity, is not ignored, or mistreated but celebrated and incorporated into your life plan.

As someone who is being personally tutored by God, take some time to write down any questions you may have for your Teacher. What answers have been elusive to you? Allow yourself enough time to listen for the answers, as your Teacher always gives them.

Practice:

Read Psalm 25:4-5 and meditate on the truth that God is a loving and patient teacher who guides us in His ways. Ask Him to reveal any areas in your life where you need His instruction and guidance.

DAY 28

God as Celebrator

> *The Lord thy God in the midst of thee*
> *is mighty; he will save, he will rejoice*
> *over thee with joy; he will rest in his*
> *love, he will joy over thee with singing.*
> *Zephaniah 3:17 KJV*

One of the most sacred revelations about the person of God we can ever come into is understanding God as the Supreme Celebrator of us. God is in a good mood. Today, God is rejoicing and dancing over you with singing. God is genuinely happy, especially about you. Take a moment and take that in. Can you see a smile on the face of God today? Can you see God rejoicing and dancing over you with singing? Can you hear the voice of God singing your name?

If it's feeling weird to consider, remember we've been programmed to believe God is an austere God-man in the sky who has no emotions, and if He does, it's anger. But this cannot be true because you were created in the image of God. And you have a range of emotions, and the healthiest emotions for our bodies are joy, peace, and love. Sounds like the Kingdom, right?

So if the Kingdom of God is love, joy, and peace in the Holy Spirit, how can God be experiencing anything other than those emotions about you? Think about it.

Practice:

Read Zephaniah 3:17 and meditate on the truth that God rejoices over you with singing. Put on your favorite feel-good songs and dance for at least 30 minutes. Celebrate, rejoice, and dance. Act like God.

DAY 29

God as Deliverer

> *I have told you these things, so that in me you may have peace. In this world you will have trouble. But take heart! I have overcome the world.*
>
> *John 16:33*

Always and forever, God is at war with your fears. Fear is the absence of the awareness of the presence of God. So, God's war with your fears is God's desire to be seen and recognized in your life as your greatest Lover (1 John 4:18).

Love and fear are the two root causes of all the gamut of emotions we experience. And perfect love casts out all fear. So God's deliverance isn't stepping in and removing people, things or circumstances. Instead, it is God making His presence known on the inside of you.

As a New Testament believer, you can take comfort in knowing that God has taken away all of your reasons to fear in the sacrifice of Jesus. God has overcome this world for you through Christ, and it is your faith in Jesus and God's great display of

His presence that delivers you from all fear, including the fear of going to hell for being LGBTQ+ (1 John 5:4-5).

Practice:

In your journal, write down all the old beliefs you have had about deliverance as an LGBTQ+ person, and surrender those old beliefs to God. Then, write down new beliefs you're going to embrace based upon today's meditation. Read those out loud to yourself at least three times today.

DAY 30

Jesus is the Word of God.

*In the beginning was the Word,
and the Word was with God,
and the Word was God.
John 1:1*

God cannot be separated from His Word. This is why making the Bible the "word of God" has been so damaging. Jesus alone is the perfect Word of God, not the Bible. While the Bible contains valuable insights and teachings, it is important to remember that every single word in the Bible does not necessarily reflect the character of God. It is a book about a nation's experience and interpretations of that experience with their perception of God.

The only accurate representation we have of God is in the person of Jesus. Jesus Christ is God. He is the exact representation of God. When we see and hear Jesus, we hear God. As Bill Johnson, a popular pastor, has said, "Jesus is perfect" theology. And although we may not agree with his ministry, this statement is one of the truest things we've heard.

As you continue in your journey of knowing and experiencing God, you have a perfect example in Christ Jesus. The most magnificent gift God has given us is Jesus Christ as our mirror.

God did not testify through Jesus of Himself to make you feel inferior, but to elevate your esteem of yourself.

"But whoever looks intently into the perfect law that gives freedom, and continues in it—not forgetting what they have heard, but doing it—they will be blessed in what they do." (James 1:25) Jesus Christ is the perfect law of liberty!

Practice:

Take 5 minutes today to look in the mirror. As you are looking into the mirror, focus on your eyes. See Jesus Christ, the exalted Spiritual Being, the Jesus of Revelations 1, looking through your eyes at you. Follow with 10 minutes of journaling about your experience.

DAY 31

Words of Love

> *As the Father has loved me, so have I loved you. Now remain in my love. If you keep my commands, you will remain in my love, just as I have kept my Father's commands and remain in his love. I have told you this so that my joy may be in you and that your joy may be complete. My command is this: Love each other as I have loved you.*
>
> *John 15:9-12*

If God is love, and He is, then Jesus must be a never-ending proclamation of love. He speaks to your spirit, and His Spirit communicates the reality of love. God the Parent, the Child, and the Spirit all speak in one language, and that language is love.

This is the most important way to determine if the voice you hear is the voice of God. If the words you hear in your heart do not inspire you to feel loved or experience joy, then it is not the voice of God. With so many voices in religion, from our parents, and from society, it can be confusing to discern if it's God, the devil, you, or your pastor. However, the formula is simple: if it's loving, it's God. If it's not loving, then it's not God.

In case your thoughts are jumping up to say, "What about when I do something wrong?" God loves you into repentance. As the scripture says, "Or do you think lightly of the riches of His kindness and tolerance and patience, not knowing that the kindness of God leads you to repentance?" (Romans 2:4)

Love is the only commandment spoken to you that you can use to judge whether or not you are being a "good Christian." It's not about who you are dating or conforming to gender stereotypes. The measure of your behavior is simple–are you loving others as Christ has loved you? No other rubric is necessary to judge your actions. And the process is straightforward. Receive God's love, and then let it pour out of you to others.

Practice:

Write a love letter to yourself from Jesus. Sit down and ask the Lord to share His loving heart for you. Write for as long as you need, without judgment. Then take a step back and cross out everything that is not loving. Rewrite it with only the loving parts. Keep it to read whenever you start to doubt that God loves you.

DAY 32

Words of Inclusion

> *I am the good shepherd; I know my sheep and my sheep know me— just as the Father knows me and I know the Father—and I lay down my life for the sheep. I have other sheep that are not of this sheep pen. I must bring them also. They too will listen to my voice, and there shall be one flock and one shepherd.*
> *John 10:14-16*

Jesus spoke words of inclusion, not exclusion. He came to save the world, not just one nation. All nations of the world, as in the popular children's song, "Jesus loves the little children, red and yellow, black and white, they are precious in His sight." Let's add to that, "Lesbian, gay, bisexual, trans, asexual, aromantic, and every human in between. Jesus loves the nations of the world!"

Jesus intentionally spoke about inclusion; you were never forgotten and always included by Him, the perfect image of God. He always had and has His eye on the lost sheep and will always leave the 99 to go pick you up on His shoulders to return you to His fold.

It's easy to forget this when we get lost in the religion and theology of Christianity. However, when we remember that Jesus is perfect theology, it's easy to see how we've always been included from the very beginning!

"But go and learn what this means: 'I desire mercy, not sacrifice.' For I have not come to call the righteous, but sinners." (Matthew 9:13)

Practice:

Take 20-30 minutes today to meditate and journal about Jesus' constant and forever inclusion of you. How intentional God shows Himself to be through the person of Jesus, that He would leave the 99 to go after the 1. Accept it, believe it, and surrender to it today.

DAY 33

Words of Forgiveness

> *Jesus said, "Father, forgive them, for they do not know what they are doing." And they divided up his clothes by casting lots.*
> *Luke 23:34*

Let's have a slightly different conversation today. Let's not talk about God forgiving us, and let's talk about us forgiving others.

I know you've been hurt by the words and actions of others about your identity. It may have been intentional or unintentional by the person. It may have been someone you loved or a stranger online. It may have come as a shock, or maybe you expected it because of previous interactions with that person. It may not even be one person, but a group of people, like the church.

No matter who it is, how they hurt you, or when they hurt you, forgiveness is required. I know, that's a tough one. Let me share a statistic with you that might help. According to "The Forgiveness Project" by Michael Barry, 61% of cancer patients have chronic levels of unforgiveness. You see, forgiveness is a requirement for you and not the person/people involved.

Jesus speaks words of forgiveness in our lives, not only towards us but as empowerment for our own forgiveness of others. You are empowered to release all the emotional and spiritual debts others have in your life. You are authorized to release them and trust the healing of the pain they caused to God.

Practice:

You can do this. Write a list of the names of the people who have hurt you in your journey of making peace with your faith and sexuality. Next to each name, write down how what they did hurt you, using only the emotions their actions or inactions caused. Like this, "X made me feel (insert emotion)." Next, out loud, say, "I forgive X for making me feel (insert emotion). I release them from the pain they've caused me." And then ask God to fill the place in your heart with love, peace, and joy.

DAY 34

Words of Encouragement

> *I have told you these things, so that in me you may have peace. In this world you will have trouble. But take heart! I have overcome the world.*
> *John 16:33*

Life can get really hard at times and in those times it's easy to think Jesus is not speaking. Religion may have caused you to believe God is silent during hard times to test your faith. That is a lie. God is speaking through Jesus and saying, "take heart!" In other translations it says "Be of good cheer, I have overcome this world for you!"

Jesus is always present to help us have a good attitude in hard times. An attitude of faith because He's handled it for us. And in 1 John 5:4 it says, " for everyone born of God overcomes the world. This is the victory that has overcome the world, even our faith."

Jesus' words of encouragement is not an invitation to false or toxic positivity. It is a substantial offer based upon the real work of Christ, who did in fact overcome this world. And did it in such spectacular fashion that you and I can be of good cheer no matter what is going on around us. No matter what the external world has going on, we can be of good cheer on the inside.

Practice:

Take John 16:33 and write it down on a small piece of paper. Keep it in your wallet, purse, or pocket for the day. Whenever you see the paper, take a moment to read the scripture and let its power sink deep into your heart. Allow Christ's words to encourage you and give you peace as you face life's challenges.

DAY 35

Words of Humility

> *Now that I, your Lord and Teacher, have washed your feet, you also should wash one another's feet. I have set you an example that you should do as I have done for you.*
> *John 13:14-15*

Notice in the beginning of our verse today, Jesus is agreeing with what God says about Him. He's not denying that He is the Lord or that He is the Teacher. Society would tell you that someone who starts off a statement about service by announcing their title is not being humble, but arrogant. So, what is happening here with Jesus?

Jesus' definition and practice of humility is agreeing with what God says about Him. We often think true humility means groveling or being a doormat for others to walk on. Beloved, this is not humility; it is actually pride. Whenever we are focused on ourselves in comparison with others, we are being self-centered, which is pride. So, whether you are viewing others as better than yourself or viewing them as worse than you, it is all pride.

True humility is agreeing with what God says about you and, with that knowledge and acceptance, serving others in all of your glory. This is true humility. Therefore, when God humbles you, it is never to tear you down; it is always to raise you up to your true divine identity. So, you can peacefully pray without fear, "God, please humble me."

Practice:

That prayer is frightful, but only for people who don't know the true character of God. Let that be your prayer today. "God, show me who I really am. Let me see myself through your eyes and help me to accept, believe, and surrender to my divine reality." As always, journal what you see and experience.

DAY 36

Words of Faith

> *So Jesus answered and said to them, "Have faith in God. For assuredly, I say to you, whoever says to this mountain, 'Be removed and be cast into the sea,' and does not doubt in his heart, but believes that those things he says will be done, he will have whatever he says. Therefore I say to you, whatever things you ask when you pray, believe that you receive them, and you will have them."*
> *Mark 11:22-24 NKJV*

Faith is natural to us as human beings. We have faith in all sorts of things, like the chair we're sitting on or the floor holding up the chair. We have faith that there will be oxygen for the next breath we take. We have so much faith in these things that we don't even think about it. But that's not what this verse is speaking about.

This verse is talking about having the faith of God. It's speaking to us as beings made in the image of God, whose words have creative power. It is speaking to us as little "g" gods. Jesus is telling us that we have the same power in our words that God has in His words, if we would believe it. Basically, Jesus is saying, "I'm not special. You can do what I do if you would believe it."

This is incredible because we are no longer just talking about Jesus' words, but about the power of Jesus' words. And that same power is available to us! Our words of faith have the same power as the words of Jesus! This is when being a Christian gets really fun!

Practice:

Think about a time when you prayed and received an answer to your prayer. Take time to remember how you felt when you prayed, what happened after the prayer, and how you received the answer. Be as detailed as possible. If this has happened more than once, take 30 minutes to try and remember all of the times. Use this as a memorial whenever you start to doubt in your heart.

DAY 37

Words of Peace

> *Peace I leave with you; my peace I give you. I do not give to you as the world gives. Do not let your hearts be troubled and do not be afraid.*
> *John 14:27*

According to Jesus, there is never a reason to be afraid or to allow your heart to be troubled. You have the peace of God always with you. And as a Christian, the peace of God is within you. This is the peace that surpasses all understanding. (Philippians 4:7)

This same peace always accompanies the words of Jesus, Holy Spirit, or God the Parent when they speak to you. Even when Jesus brings correction to your actions, His words will be filled with peace. Here's why; because Jesus' words will always bring you back to the truth. The truth is that you are unconditionally loved by God. And this love will never be a reason to put you in fear or cause your heart to be troubled.

Remember this today and always. God's words to you as a Queer Christian will always be accompanied by peace. If peace is not present, it is not God, even if it is a pastor, prophet, or teacher.

If they have a "word" for you that produces fear and causes your heart to be troubled, it is not God.

Practice:

In your journal, write a description of what the voice of God has sounded like before and what it is supposed to sound like. Include the emotions the voice of God is supposed to produce in your heart. Meditate on it during the day and ask God to add more feeling words to how His voice sounds.

DAY 38

Words of Wholeness

> *You are already clean because of the word I have spoken to you. Remain in me, as I also remain in you. No branch can bear fruit by itself; it must remain in the vine. Neither can you bear fruit unless you remain in me.*
> *John 15:3-4*

The words of Jesus cleanse our hearts from shame, condemnation, and guilt. It removes all of our need to perform and be perfect for God. It rinses away all of the religious programs we have set up in our hearts and minds that keep us feeling separated from God. You are whole and complete in Him. (John 15:3)

So you can rest, knowing the work of cleansing your heart is already done. If you have heard Jesus and believed Him about who He is, your faith has already cleansed you. Your heart is not desperately wicked. Your desires can be trusted and followed. (Psalm 37:4)

You are not only whole in Christ, but you are fruitful in Him. And you bear good fruit! You can trust the power of the words of Christ as much as He trusts His own words. And if He says the words, He has spoken have cleansed you, you can trust it with all of your being.

Practice:

Today, while you shower or take a bath, picture the water as the words of Jesus cleansing you. Take your time and really imagine all of the amazing truths of God washing over your body. Journal about the experience when you are finished.

DAY 39

Words of Freedom

> *Then you will know the truth,*
> *and the truth will set you free.*
> *John 8:32*

Jesus came to set us free for the sake of freedom alone. (Galatians 5:1) It was not for any other reason - not to love others better, to serve God, or to fulfill any other role in life. Jesus came to set us free because freedom is our birthright.

We attain this freedom by becoming intimate with the words of Christ, which are truth. By knowing and experiencing in the depths of our beings the truths of God, we experience this freedom.

Your freedom is free; it only requires time, your undivided attention, and your commitment to seeking truth. You must have a desire and hunger for truth and pursue it with all you have, expecting that it is available and plentiful for you. The truth is not hidden; there is no maze you must navigate to find it. It is here, it is for you, and it is your freedom.

Practice:

Take 20-30 minutes to journal about the time you have sincerely devoted to seeking truth. Is it your true desire? If it is not, ask God to help you develop a desire for truth and freedom. Then commit to setting aside time to intimately experience truth in the words of Jesus Christ.

DAY 40

Words of Oneness

> *I have given them the glory that you gave me, that they may be one as we are one—I in them and you in me—so that they may be brought to complete unity. Then the world will know that you sent me and have loved them even as you have loved me.*
>
> *John 17:22-23*

Beloved, you and Christ Jesus are one. All of who you are is beautifully engulfed in Christ, and all of who Christ is powerfully exists and abides in you. You are flesh of His flesh and bone of His bones.

You are never separated from God. Wherever you are, God is. God has made His, Her, Their home in you. It is the most beautiful union. This union is the blueprint and pattern for all of your life. This ecstatic union with God is a reminder that you were made to feel good, that life is supposed to feel good, that joy is supposed to be your default, and that being perfectly loved is the bare minimum.

You were created for this Union. All of you was made to live intertwined within God, your Creator. There's no space between you and your Divine. This is the stuff dreams are made of. This is your reality always and forever. It is eternal. It is beautiful. It is all yours!

Colossians 2:9-10 confirms, "For in Christ all the fullness of the Deity lives in bodily form, and in Christ, you have been brought to fullness."

Practice:

Take a moment to breathe all of that in. Read over each statement slowly and really breathe in every word. This one truth has the ability to transform your entire life.

About the Author

As the founder of the Confidently Queer coaching program, Yeamah Logan is a sought-after author, coach, and international speaker dedicated to empowering LGBTQ+ people to live fully authentic lives while deepening their spiritual connection with God. With over 10 years of experience in the field, Yeamah Logan has become a trusted resource for those seeking guidance and support on their journey towards self-discovery and spiritual growth. Through her work, Yeamah has touched the lives of countless individuals, helping them to heal, thrive, and embrace their truest selves.

For more information or to work with Coach Yeamah visit www.confidentlyqueer.com

www.ingramcontent.com/pod-product-compliance
Lightning Source LLC
Chambersburg PA
CBHW070438010526
44118CB00014B/2099